SOUL SEEKER
Lyrics of Love Lost and Gained

By
William Armstrong

If you are interested in producing or performing any of these song lyrics, please contact me at
www.armstrong40510@yahoo.com

Banned

No more tears. I'm done, we're through.
I can sleep, no dreams of you.
I won't beg that you let me go.
'cause now I'm done. Thought you should know.
I pray the scars you left don't show.

I've closed the door to this heart in me,
Turned the lock, lost the key.
Time for me to make a new start
You been banned from my shattered heart.
And, I'm much better now that we're apart.
And, I'm much better now that we're apart.

I had hopes that when we met,
You'd be the fit for me, and yet
Our life as one was not enough.
When I heard the news, the truth was rough.
With someone else you shared your love.

Grieving that we were no more,
The waves crashing on an empty shore.
No-one to understand my pain,
My cries were wasted and in vain.
No ocean could my tears contain.

I've closed the door to this heart in me,
Turned the lock, lost the key.
Time for me to make a new start

You been banned from my shattered heart.
And, I'm much better now that we're apart.
And, I'm much better now that we're apart.

I feared that all my hope was gone,
And I could never carry on.
Feeling lost in my own life,
Happiness replaced by strife,
And darkness quenched my soul's light.

I don't regret, we were not wrong.
The pain you left has made me strong.
And, don't you worry, heart of my past,
I've found real peace I know will last.
This strength is deep and true steadfast.

I'll never again feel lost love's ache
The soul I've found, the love I make,
It leaves me ready to believe
A brighter day is what I see.
This perfect love I've found is me.

I've closed the door to this heart in me,
Turned the lock, lost the key.
Time for me to make a new start
You been banned from my shattered heart.
And, I'm much better now that we're apart.
And, I'm much better now that we're apart.

Dancing Out Loud

We fight a rumba of shouting
We whisper a tango of love
Our dance moves are haltingly spoken
And answered with kisses or shoves

Our bed is a dance floor of passion
Where we salsa, our hips move in time
To the beat of our hearts,
And the tune of our cries
Our ballet is one of excitement sublime

We sway to the music of loving
An embrace of words when we speak
Our arguments, a terrible two-step
A mambo that leaves us tired and weak

But then, our ballroom awaits
And our caper out loud carries on
To keep us in tune
With our souls' dance steps
May love's music continue loud and strong
May love's music continue loud and strong

We sway to the music of loving
An embrace of words when we speak
Our arguments, a terrible two-step
A mambo that leaves us tired and weak

I Cannot Wait

What do I feel inside my heart?

Is it love or the ache when we're apart?
Without your smile inside my mind,
My world is lonely and unkind,
My soul is trapped and my heart is blind.

Thoughts of you race through my mind
And see me through my day.
I cannot wait until tonight
And tell you all I want to say.
In your arms, my cares melt away.

Your eyes, they tell me how you feel.
And say to me our love is real.
Your lips, they call me to your arms
Your touch is soft, your breath is warm.
You keep my hungry soul from harm.

I wake to thoughts of you each day,
Your face still takes my breath away.
When daily cares have left me numb,
I anticipate the night to come,
When I'll feel my body's thrilling hum.

Thoughts of you race through my mind
And see me through my day.
I cannot wait until tonight
And tell you all I want to say.
In your arms, my cares melt away.

My day goes by, the hours slow,
But all my nerves ignite to know

That when the busy day is done,
And with the setting of the sun,
We'll be together, joined as one.

I cannot wait until tonight,
When loving you will feel so right.
The thought of us makes my heart race,
I cannot wait to see your face
And gather you in my embrace.

Thoughts of you race through my mind
And see me through my day.
I cannot wait until tonight
And tell you all I want to say.
In your arms, my cares melt away.
Your love melts all my cares away.

My Tide

My love is like the ocean, baby
Waves of desire crash over me
My love is like the ocean, baby
My heart swells with thoughts of you and
me

You found me on the sand despairing
Lost and lonely, not wanting to try
You found me on the sand in sadness
The sand of grief, the sand of 'why'

I ride the tide from 'me' to 'us'

My soul, it flows from blue to green
I ride the tide from 'me' to 'us'
Devotion's storm leaves me serene

You found me on the sand despairing
Lost and lonely, not wanting to try
You found me on the sand in sadness
The sand of grief, the sand of 'why'

Excitement ripples throughout my body
It pounds my soul, I long for you
Excitement ripples throughout my body
I swim it 'til our next rendezvous

You warm me like an ocean breeze
Your body leaves me soaking wet
You warm me like an ocean breeze
I'm caught in your sweet passion's net

You found me on the sand despairing
Lost and lonely, not wanting to try
You found me on the sand in sadness
The sand of grief, the sand of 'why'

Our love is like the ocean, baby
Set sail with me 'til the end of time
Our life is like the ocean, baby
Wide and deep, a thing sublime

My Mistake

A long time now, so many tears
Mired in loss, so many years
I let you go, I was too young
Clouds of regret, hiding the sun

Can't turn back time, there's no rewind
Memories of us always in my mind
Mists of 'forget', inadequate
Mirrors my heart, no relief yet

I tell myself to let me go
My search for love is moving slow
I beg myself to let me be
So I can find a brand new me

Singing all my sorrows gone
Is wasted time, it feels so wrong
One new start is all I need
To prove to someone how I feel

Mistakes in life in years gone past
Proved our love's the one to last
Another chance, my heart, my soul
Forever love, my only goal

I tell myself to let me go
My search for love is moving slow
I beg myself to let me be
So I can find a brand new me

If you hear my cry from where

I drown in my sea of despair
Come rescue me and lift me up
I'll prove that I can rise above

I tell myself to let me go
My search for love is moving slow
I beg myself to let me be
So I can find a brand new me

Golden Stone

Still, my searching continues on
Guided by my lasting hope
I know my longing isn't wrong
My loneliness has taken a toll

Calling on my heart to find
My life's true settled soul
I tear down walls that fill my mind
And move me towards my wanted goal

My dreams rub raw. I don't want to try
My heart sits like a golden stone
I fight so love doesn't say 'goodbye'
And leave me bereft, cold and alone

Doing all I can to live
Certain my heart will never be
I know and want what I have to give
And I hold on tight, until you find me

When I find you, then I'll know
The clouds will finally lift
I'll have the love I need to show
My loneliness was worth the gift

My dreams rub raw, I don't want to try
My heart sits like a golden stone
I fight so love doesn't say 'goodbye'
To leave me bereft, cold and alone

Can your eyes see who I am?
Do you recognize true love?
A simple, basic strength which stands
To build our world, a sheltered home

And so, I keep my hope alive
See where we go and what we do
To be one heart and soul and mind
I take the chance with you

My dreams rub raw, I don't want to try
My heart sits like a golden stone
I fight so love doesn't say 'goodbye'
To leave me bereft, cold and alone

Seasons Gone

You started out the perfect one
We met and there was magic,
Laughter and excited talk
Who know it'd end so tragic

Every day we grew and smiled
Each hour was for the future
We learned to take it slowly, love
To know each other, true and sure

Our friends, they smiled and toasted us
Our bodies hummed in bliss
Our days were sun and joy and deep
Our nights were one long tender kiss

Gone forever, I'm all tears
My life's a puzzle, shattered
Empty, broken, frightened me
I'm all alone and nothing matters

Waking with you by my side
I didn't want to leave
The bed was warm and so were you
My contentment was beyond belief

My skin, it thrilled at every touch
Your skin made me feel so alive
Your breath was like an autumn breeze
My body hummed from deep inside

And then, one day, it all went wrong
Your phone, it rang; I answered
Another voice spoke soft your name
And held my heart in ransom

Dark clouds, they started rolling in
The day I found your note
The bed was cold, the closet bare
I shivered with my loss of hope

Gone forever, I'm all tears
My life's a puzzle, shattered
Empty, broken, frightened me
I'm all alone and nothing matters

Suddenly, the songs we sang
Were screams of pain and black despair
And when the smoke had finally cleared
Your gentle breath was no longer there

And so, long life, I see no more
My heart, a nightmare in a cage
All is one, my one is gone
Please close the book, don't turn the page

The sun, it rises one last time
I see the day in sad relief
I'm going home forever now
No more joy, no more grief

Gone forever, I'm all tears
My life's a puzzle, shattered
Empty, broken, frightened me
I'm all alone and nothing matters

The Climb

Picking up the pieces
Of my lonely, empty life
Recent battles, hours of pain
Days of screaming, awful strife

The hope I found from my last love
Had misted in the night
The future I had dreamed of
Had faded with each fight

Where to go? What to do?
All the questions came
Who would care enough to love
And help me move on past the pain?

I started to breathe easier
I said 'goodbye' with relief
Knowing yesterday was gone
I started growing past my grief

It's true, that day I saw you there
Your warm, inviting smile
You took those first exciting steps
Towards 'us'; me stopping all the while

We talked and laughed, I must admit
I fought against my doubt
My mind said 'no', my worry, too
I knew my heart kept hope slowed down

You prevailed, you understood
And made me feel alive
You let me in and drew me close
You called my bluff, I calmed my mind

Where to go? What to do?
All the questions came
Who would care enough to love
And help me move on past the pain?

Because of you, the past is gone
And 'now' is where I want to be
Simple things, they keep us strong
A love for us is what I see

Where to go? What to do?
All the questions came
You would care enough to love
And help me move on past the pain?

The Third

We made the perfect couple
At least, we looked the part
Smiling and laughing, kissing and loving
That's the way it always starts

The envy of all of our friends
We turned heads wherever we went
And whether in public or private
Our time was perfectly spent

We seized the moment and took our chance
Why did we go so wrong?
All of our hopes of 'us' forever
Shattered, and now the pain lasts too long

Souls in the light, we knew what to do
Building our life, protecting our hearts
Falling in love every day

Then it happened, out of the blue
Another entered our life
One of us thought other would not
Find out that our flower had died

We seized the moment and took our chance
Why did we go so wrong?
All of our hopes of 'us' together
Shattered, and now the pain lasts too long

And then, the screaming, it started
Of anger and hurt and betrayal
Tears, heartache, all of 'us' lost
'I'm sorry' was said to no avail

This wasn't a game we were playing
The pain was real and cut deep
Moving through life, dazed and bereft
Love was no more, now only grief

So, what to do, where to go?

Can I trust my heart to another?
I won't accept blame, I don't own the shame
Memories of you in the arms of a lover

We seized the moment and took our chance
Why did we go so wrong?
All of our hopes of 'us' together
Shattered, and the pain lasts too long
Shattered, and the tears just go on

<u>Who Needs It?</u>

Sentimental sugar cane
Love song, sappy sweetness
Stir some into my heart-brew
Mix some golden with my greenness

Watching couples cringe together
Weeping "Love me for all time.
Don't you ever let me go."
Makes me laugh until I cry

I don't need to give away
My strength and who I am
To someone else and watch them crush
My body, heart and soul

I don't mind the tears at night
My bed is cold and I'm alone
Why do I cry for someone else
To join me, body, heart and soul?

All these words of "Love me, do"
They make me smile, I'm too smart
To give into all those lies
And give another one my heart

All that kissing, keep it all
I'm just fine. I'm okay
Hugging, holding, gifts and words
I won't give myself away

Stop your trying, I won't give in
Cupid's arrow's off the mark
I can move through 'day-to-day'
Without a constant grab at my heart

I don't need to give away
My strength and who I am
To someone else and watch them crush
My body, heart and soul

I don't mind the tears at night
My bed is cold and I'm alone
Why do I cry for someone else
To join me, body, heart and soul?

You say "I'm crazy. Love's the way
To find life's happiest true."
But, I don't think you're right, you see
I can handle my mood, when blue

Going to find you?

Waiting here
Always stare
At my heart
Searching

Don't you want me?
Don't you need me?
Why are we lost?
All we need is 'us'

Come with me
Be with me
Only me
Baby!

See our love
Rise above
All the haters
Baby!

Yeah!
I want you!
Baby, yeah!
Yeah!
I need you!
Baby, now!

Love is all
Everything

So, don't keep at it, let me be
I know what makes me happy
It's not your syrup-sweet connection
A life of weakness, lame and sappy

I don't need to give away
My strength and who I am
To someone else and watch them crush
My body, heart and soul

I don't mind the tears at night
My bed is cold and I'm alone
Why do I cry for someone else
To join me, body, heart and soul?
To save me, body, heart and soul?

Solitaria

I sit alone
Eat alone
Sleep alone
Always wondering

Where are you?
Who are you?
When are you
Going to save me?

Why do I?
Who am I?
When am I

What I sing
For you!

Heart and soul
My only goal
What I bring
For us!

Find me here
Wandering where
We will meet
Someday

Yeah!
I want you!
Baby, yeah!
Yeah!
I need you!
Baby, now!
I need you now!
I want you now
Yeah!

Time Enough

Listen to me sing my lonely song
Every note a crystal teardrop
No one to see, nothing to feel
Grief for time passing has got to stop

Needing your love is who I am

Wanting to give mine to you
Seeing the two of us holding 'us' close
And making a future, safe and true

Don't look away, find me today
Know that my love-light is shining
Warm in its glow, show me your own
Let's end our separate pining

Calling for you through days of me
My soul is tired and beaten
Every hour is long and drawn-out
The challenge is, how will I meet them?

When I'm at home, sad and alone
All of my wishes are met
Except for my dream of being with you
A dream I haven't fulfilled yet

Don't look away, find me today
Know that my love-light is shining
Warm in its glow, show me your own
Let's end our separate pining

Nothing is certain, don't draw the curtain
You and I can still be
All of our life, our love can grow stronger
Answer my cry and you'll see

Don't look away, find me today
Know that our love-light is shining

Warm in its glow, show me your own
Let's end our desperate pining

You Finally Did It

You finally did it, you found a chance
To give your love to another
You took all our moments of perfect love
And saw them destroyed by a lover

Nothing was left, you made quite sure
That all our time was a waste
You didn't mean to, you said "a mistake."
Forbidden love, you'd wanted to taste

You tried to smile, it just was in fun
Your boredom, the cause, you said
But soon your smile faded away
When I told you all of my love was dead

I wouldn't play this game with you
It isn't how love should be
Your trifling times are not what I want
And now it's too late for you to see

The blame is yours, I won't own the pain
I tried to see your way
I listened and wanted to see it be past
But, there was no loving in what you would
say

So we are gone, nothing is left
Your lover has said "go away."
And now, we're both alone with our pain
My search for another begins today

I wouldn't play this game with you
It isn't how love should be
Your trifling times are not what I want
And now it's too late for you to see

The Upside

After years of waiting
Calling out your name
All my hopes have been answered
My loneliness has proved in vain

Finally, you're by my side
We are the perfect pair
Love has long been absent
The void is no longer there

The sun has lightened our dark days
And driven back the night
Our days, unburdened, unafraid
Are no longer a lonely fight

We celebrate a newfound way
To see our starting spring
Hand-in-hand, heart-to-heart
We find new songs of love to sing

Is it real, this smile I wear
That will not fade away?
Is it true, how my heart leaps
With every word you say?

We live our separate lives, for sure
But when we're back together
It's so clear to both of us
That we are two as one forever

Nothing feels like when you're close
Your skin, your hair, your kiss
I wrap myself in your embrace
Each day, anew, it all begins

And so, my love, step-by-step
We're closer to eternity
We loosed the knot, unlocked the chains
And found our soul's serenity

In The Choosing

I'm trapped between two hearts
Both I meet with love
One is strong and safe and warm
The other, risk, excitement, fun

One is always there for me
I never have to worry
If I make a bad mistake

I never have to say "I'm sorry"

The other meets my forceful needs
When my life needs a spark
To lift me out of boredom's grip
This choice will someday break my heart

I am torn by guilty choice
I'm told I should not play
With selfish wishes, cheating games
It only ends in a painful way

Solid, strong, trusting love
Is what I give to one
And in return, I get it back
A caring heart that's never done

Quick and loose and non-stop life
I find within the other
Smiling, laughing, moving fast
My irresponsible lover

I am torn by guilty choice
I'm told I should not play
With selfish wishes, cheating games
It only ends in a painful way

And so, I'm trapped between two hearts
And have to make a choice
Between a love that heals my soul
And one of screaming, pointless noise

Single

Where I stand, looking back
What I know for sure
Is that my life is missing you
Your heart and soul, strong and pure

So much time without your love
Too many years bereft
So many answers yet to know
Too many questions left

The past is gone, time's flown away
I watch my life without you
I bid 'goodbye' as days fly past
What could have been and all I lose

How much better would my life
Have been if we were one
Our two souls joined together
Shining brighter than the sun

The sands of time are blowing past
They make a lonely desert
Dark and dry and empty now
All I do is sadly yearn

The past is gone, time's flown away
I watch my life without you
I bid 'goodbye' as days fly past

What could have been and all I lose

I let you go and made my way
Among the happy couples
To watch and know what could have been
A life without this endless struggle

All I hope, it's not too late
For me to fine the one
Who lifts me from this empty life
And wraps me in love's warming sun

www.ingramcontent.com/pod-product-compliance
Lightning Source LLC
Chambersburg PA
CBHW071449040426
42445CB00012BA/1500